DORLING KINDERSLEY *READERS*

BEGINNING
2
TO READ ALONE

Slinky, Scaly Snakes!

Written by Jennifer Dussling

DK

DK PUBLISHING, INC.

Slinky, scaly snakes
slide along the ground.

They have legless bodies
and look through unblinking eyes.

Everglades rat snake

Snakes are shiny
and can look slimy.
But they are dry
and smooth to touch.

Rattlesnake

A snake's whole body
is covered in scales.
These scales are hard and tough
like fingernails.

Snakes grow quickly,
but their skin doesn't stretch.
When a snake's skin gets too tight,
the snake has to shed it.
This is called molting.

Rock python

The snake rubs its head
on something rough like a log.
After a few minutes,
the skin begins to peel.

The shed skin
of a snake

The snake slides forward
and right out of its skin!
Underneath is a new skin.
It looks bright and shiny.
The snake keeps on growing.
Soon it will be time
to molt again.

Wait and see
When a snake is ready
to molt, its eyes turn
milky white. The snake
is almost blind for a week,
so it stays hidden.

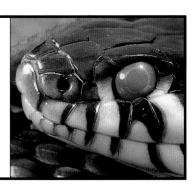

Snakes have no legs.
They move in long, slinky curves.
The ground may look smooth
but it has little bumps everywhere.
A snake pushes off the bumps
to move itself forward.

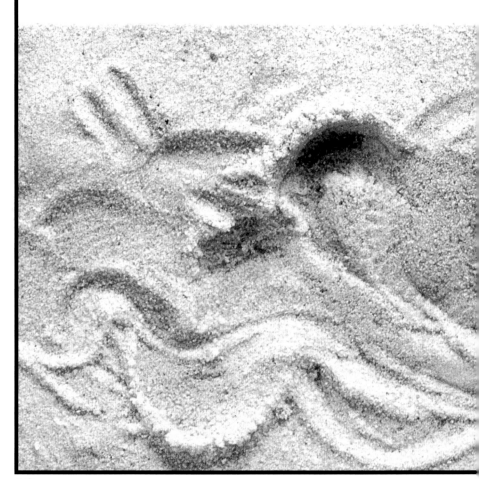

The sidewinder snake
lives in the desert.
It throws itself forward
one part at a time.
It leaves behind
wavy-looking tracks.

Eyelash viper

Not all snakes live on the ground.
Some live in trees.

Snakes may not have legs,
but they can still climb.
A snake has scales
on its belly
that are larger
than the ones on its back.
These scales grip the tree.
The snake uses
its strong muscles
to pull itself up the tree.

Boa constrictor

How are snakes born?

Some give birth to live babies.

Other snakes lay eggs.

Florida kingsnake laying eggs

Soft shell

Snake eggs
are not hard
like chicken eggs.
The shells are soft,
almost like leather.

A mother snake doesn't usually stay with her eggs.

She lays them in a soft, warm place, then she leaves them.

Soon a baby snake pokes its head out of the egg.

Then it slithers out of its shell.

Rat snake

Haitian (HAY-shun) boa

This snake is not moving.
Only its tongue flicks in and out.
It is checking for danger.

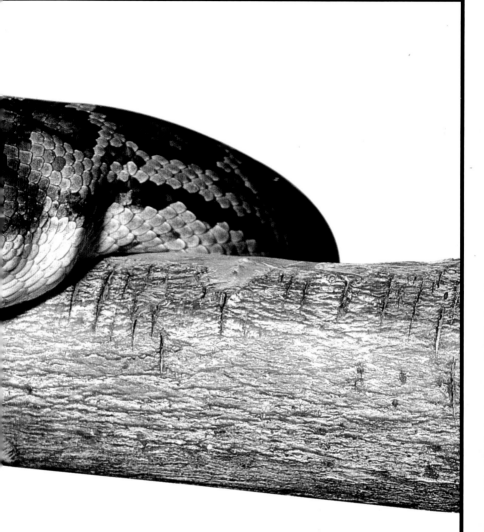

Most snakes can't see or hear well.
But they have
a strong sense of smell.
And they pick up these smells
with their tongues.

A fox meets a whipsnake

But what are snakes afraid of?

Hawks, raccoons, and foxes

like to eat snakes.

Some snakes eat other snakes.

But many snakes have ways

to fool their enemies.

Some snakes blend in
with the area around them.
This vine snake looks like
a vine hanging from a tree.

These gaboon vipers
look like fallen leaves.

Other snakes try to trick
their enemies.

The parrot snake
opens its mouth very wide
and tries to look scary.

The milk snake is harmless.
But it looks like
the deadly coral snake,
so animals stay away.

Coral snake

Milk snake

The grass snake has a great trick.
When an enemy is near,
it plays dead!

All snakes are meat-eaters.
Small snakes eat small animals
like bugs, lizards, and worms.
Some snakes eat eggs.
This snake is swallowing a bird's egg.

Egg-eating snake

The egg makes a big bulge
in the snake's body.

The egg breaks inside the snake.
Then the snake spits out the shell.

A rat makes a tasty meal
for a boa constrictor.

First the snake grabs the rat.
The snake holds on fast
with its strong jaws.

Tight squeeze
Snakes crush their prey,
but they don't break bones.
They squeeze just enough
to make the animal
stop breathing.

It wraps its long body
around and around the rat.
Then the snake starts to squeeze
tight . . . tighter . . . tighter.
Soon the rat's heart stops.

The snake opens its mouth
very, very wide.
It gulps once or twice
and swallows the rat headfirst.

A rock python swallowing a Thomson's gazelle

Big snakes eat bigger animals.
Giant pythons and boas
can be as long as a school bus.
They eat pigs, goats, and gazelles.

Big eaters

A meal can last
a long time.
Snakes like this python
have gone a whole year
without eating!

Mojave rattlesnake

Many snakes use poison
to kill their food.
The poison is stored in sacs
close to their long, sharp fangs.

The snake sticks its fangs
into the animal.

*Uracoan
rattlesnake*

The poison shoots through the
fangs and into the animal's body.
It does not take long
for the animal to die.
Then the snake swallows it whole.

Born to kill

A cobra can kill from
the minute it is born.
Just one tablespoon
of its dried poison
can kill 160,000 mice!

Can snakes hurt people?
Many can.
Here are some snakes
that can poison people.

Rattlesnake

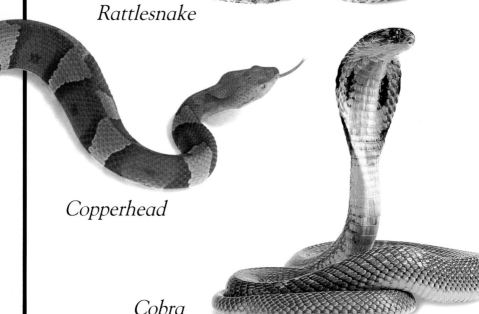

Copperhead

Cobra

But if people are bitten,
snakes can help!
Medicine is made from their poison
to treat snake bites.

Biting people better
A snake bites through
the thin covering
over a container.
Poison dripping from
its fangs is collected.

Snakes are useful in lots of ways.
They eat millions of mice
and other pests.
And they are eaten
by other hungry animals.
Our world would not be the same
without slinky, scaly snakes!

Snake Facts

Snakes are cold-blooded.
They lie in the sun to warm up
and move into the shade
to cool down.

Unlike people,
snakes never stop growing.

The world's heaviest snake
is the anaconda.
It can weigh as much
as three grown men.

The smallest snake
is the thread snake.
It is as skinny
as the lead in a pencil!

Baby snakes have a tooth
to help them break their eggs.
It falls off soon after they hatch.

It's not hard
to outrun a snake.
The fastest ones slither
at the same speed as you walk.